NELSON THOR
DRAMASCRII

THE
CROWSTARVER

Daniel Jamieson
Based on the novel by Dick King-Smith

Nelson Thornes

The right of Andy Kempe and Daniel Jamieson to be identified as authors
of this work has been asserted by them in accordance with the Copyright,
Designs and Patents Act 1988.

Published in 2013 by:
Nelson Thornes Ltd
Delta Place
27 Bath Road
CHELTENHAM
GL53 7TH
United Kingdom

13 14 15 16 17 / 10 9 8 7 6 5 4 3 2 1

A catalogue record for this book is available from the British Library

ISBN 978 1 4085 2054 3

Page make-up by OKS Prepress, India

Printed in China

CONTENTS

INTRODUCTION

Dramascripts is a series of plays for use in the English classroom and the drama studio. The plays have been written by playwrights who share a delight in live performance and the challenges it offers to actors, designers, directors and, of course, audiences.

Most of the plays in the series were written for professional companies. All are included because they tell stories and use techniques which will interest, excite and offer new insights to young people who are just coming to understand how drama works as an art form.

The range of plays in the series addresses the requirement to give students at Key Stages 3 and 4 an opportunity to study a variety of dramatic genres. The fact that they were all written for performance (and have indeed all been performed) means that they will also offer students the chance to understand how and why playscripts are different from novels. The activities presented after the script are designed to draw attention to this and to extend students' abilities in reading, writing and, of course, performing drama.

Many of the tasks invite students to use practical work to engage directly with the text or to formulate their own creative responses to its form and content. Others focus on the importance of discussing, writing and designing. Both English and drama specialists will find the series a valuable resource for promoting dramatic literacy – and simply performing the plays wouldn't be a bad thing either!

THE CROWSTARVER

'Of all the books I've written, *The Crowstarver* is one of my favourites,' Dick King-Smith told us as we sat by a crackling fire in his tiny cottage in rural Gloucestershire in 2005. In person he seemed very warm, funny and plain-speaking but not in the least sentimental. And yet, I think, the book reveals him to be a deeply emotional man, passionate in his love of animals, the countryside and its people. It was this depth of feeling that made us want to put the story on stage.

We asked what had inspired him to write the book. He told us how, when he was 18, he'd worked as a farmhand on Tytherington Farm in the Wylye Valley in Wiltshire before he went off to fight in World War Two. He talked about it fervently, as if he was suddenly seeing it all again in bright summer sunshine. And who inspired Spider Sparrow, the boy in the story? 'When I first came to this house in the sixties,' said King-Smith, 'there were five dairy farms in this little hamlet alone. The lane was often full of cows going to and from milking. Every day a boy, the son of one of the cowmen, was herding the cows back and forward. And you know the only conversation we ever had, rain or shine? "Good un!" he used to shout, as cheerful as anything. And so I used to reply, "Good un!" and we'd leave it at that.'

In the story the dawning realisation that Spider has learning difficulties is greeted in various ways, not all of them kind. But from early on it's through his gentle mastery of animals that Spider finally commands respect from everyone on Outoverdown Farm. Spider's encounters with the animal kingdom are an essential part of *The Crowstarver*. If we were going to take up the challenge of staging the book, we would have to find ways of portraying the animals. That would take all the storytelling skills we could muster. In rehearsals, different ways of showing each animal quickly felt appropriate. Some, like dogs, cats and horses, seem to possess more human personality traits.

It felt right for the actors to play these animals themselves. Others appear in large groups or off in the distance, like birds, cattle and sheep. To try and show these visibly felt like it would diminish them. The actors found that making their calls with their voices or the clatter of their wings by clapping their hands conjured them up far better. The third sort of animals are those with which Spider has fleeting, magic-feeling encounters, such as the fox and the hare. It felt like we should show these in a more special way. We ended up using puppets manipulated by the cast. The fox puppet required four actors to work but after much practice it seemed to have a life of its own.

The relationship between Spider and his mother and father is painted with great tenderness in *The Crowstarver* and that's at the heart of the story for me. When Spider is old enough for his parents to realise he's different from other children they are upset but determined to nurture his unique talents. When he's bullied, they're heartbroken. When he triumphs, they glow with modest joy. Dick King-Smith evokes the emotional rollercoaster of parenthood with particular intensity.

Finally, there is a yearning in the story for a harmony between humanity and the natural world. We can't turn back the clock and all become farmworkers once more, but our rural landscape sits patiently, waiting for us to attend to it. *The Crowstarver* makes us feel our lives would be richer for doing so.

Daniel Jamieson,
September 2012

ACKNOWLEDGEMENTS

The author and the publisher would like to thank the following for permission to reproduce material:

pp55, 56, 59 and 61 Alibi Theatre and Thomas Johnson for various opinions from the cast, crew and creative team of their production of *The Crowstarver*.

p.57 Steve Tanner, photo of hare puppet (from left: Derek Frood and Jordan Whyte) and photo of fox puppet with operators (from left: Malcolm Hamilton, Cerianne Roberts, Derek Frood, Michael Wagg and Jordan Whyte), from Theatre Alibi's production of *The Crowstarver*.

p.58 Rachel Kempe, photo of newspaper hare and fox puppets.

p.64 UK Legislation, definition of 'disabled' from 'The Children's Act', 1989, © Crown Copyright.

Every effort has been made to trace the copyright holders but if any have been inadvertently overlooked the publisher will be pleased to make the necessary arrangements at the first opportunity.

THE CHARACTERS

STORYTELLERS

TOM	a farmworker
KATHIE	his wife
EPHRAIM	the horseman
PERCY AND BILLY	farmworkers
SPIDER	a foundling
MRS YORKE	the farm owner
BOY 1	
BOY 2	
BOY 3	
GERMAN PILOT	
AUCTIONEER	
GEORGE	the auctioneer's assistant
HAULIER	
DOCTOR	

ANIMALS, portrayed by actors or puppets, include:

MOLLY	an old dog
FLOWER	a carthorse
BUCKING BRONCO	
SIS	a young dog

Also a **LAMB**, a **CUCKOO**, an **OWL**, a **CAT**, **CROWS**, a **FOX AND TWO CUBS**, a **HARE** and an entire **PACK OF FOXHOUNDS**!

FIRST PRODUCTION

The Crowstarver was commissioned and first performed by Theatre Alibi on 24 February 2006 as a co-production with the Exeter Northcott Theatre and The Lowry. It was directed by Nikki Sved.

Chris Bianchi	**TOM, BILLY, AUCTIONEER, CROWS, FOX**
Jordan Whyte	**KATHIE, EPHRAIM, GEORGE, CROWS, FOX, HARE**
Derek Frood	**PERCY, DOCTOR, BOY 1, MOLLY, BRONCO, CAT, CROWS, OWL, FOX, HARE**
Cerianne Roberts	**MRS YORKE, GERMAN PILOT, BOY 2, SIS, FLOWER, CROWS, CUCKOO, FOX**
Tom Wainwright	**SPIDER**

1 ❖ MOTHERLESS LAMB

April 1926. A moonlit night on a windswept hillside. Straggling figures walk over the brow and stop before us, listening to the night sounds. They begin to tell us a story …

STORYTELLER   The sough of the wind …

STORYTELLER   … coming over the shoulder of the Wiltshire downs …

STORYTELLER   … sweeping low across a lambing field …

STORYTELLER   … 'til it meets a stout, stone wall …

STORYTELLER   … the lambing pen on Outoverdown Farm.

STORYTELLER   Inside this, ewes and their new lambs …

Lambs cry. Ewes call back to them.

STORYTELLER   … and the shepherd's hut, safe from the west wind's buffeting.   10

A storm lantern sheds a golden glow.

Inside the hut, a shepherd, Tom Sparrow, feeding a motherless lamb.

TOM   Enough?

LAMB   Baaa.

TOM   Sure?

LAMB   Baaaa.

TOM   Go on then …

Tom *lays the lamb in a cardboard box and settles to sleep beside it.*   20

MOLLY   Woof!

STORYTELLER   Tom's dog, Molly.

TOM	Sweet dreams, Molly.
	Tom pats Molly and she lays her head on her paws.
STORYTELLER	They snatched what sleep they could at lambing time. All quiet now. Everything in its place.
STORYTELLER	Wait.
	A figure approaches with a shawl round her head, carrying something tightly.
	Along the drove from the valley road a girl comes, striving against the wind, carrying a bundle.
	She disappears into a lambing pen then backs out without the bundle. Just for a moment, she hesitates.
	And off again, arms empty.
	Only the wind remains. But now a thin wail comes from the bundle. Molly hears it straightaway.
MOLLY	WOOF!
TOM	What's up, Molly? Fox about, is there?
	Tom puts on his coat, takes the lamp and goes out of the hut. The wind and the wailing are louder now. Molly runs ahead and barks into the pen, wagging her tail. Tom picks up the bundle and takes it back to the hut. Molly noses inquisitively as Tom opens the dirty white shawl. Inside it lies a newborn baby boy. Tom holds him up, turning him this way and that, examining him as he would a new lamb.
	You're a poor little rat, you are, my lad …
	The baby cries louder. Tom holds him close. There's a note in the shawl, which Tom glances at.
	Looks like your mum's ditched you.
	He reaches for the lamb's bottle.
LAMB	Baaa.

30

40

50

TOM   Wait your turn.

After a cursory wipe of the teat, **Tom** *feeds the baby with the bottle.*

Come on, get it down you, there's a good boy ...

Ah dear, Molly, I shoulda loved a son.

A kind-looking, ruddy-cheeked woman approaches with a basket.

STORYTELLER   Kathie Sparrow comes up the drove now, Tom's wife, bringing his breakfast. Lambing time is a lonely time for her, with no child for company.   60

Kathie *goes into the hut.*

KATHIE   Tom!

Tom *shows her the note.*

'Please save this lamb.'

Kathie *takes the baby from* **Tom** *and holds him close, then they walk away down to their cottage.*

2 ❖ OUTOVERDOWN

STORYTELLER	By the next day, everyone on Outoverdown Farm and in the village knew that the Sparrows were looking after an abandoned baby.	1
	In the farm stables, **Ephraim***, the horseman, sweeps the cobbles.*	
EPHRAIM	The mother must be one o' they girls from town. Father prob'ly one o' they squaddies …	
	Percy Pound *eases his bad leg, and frowns at his pocket watch.*	
PERCY	Hmmm. Daresay.	
	Billy Butt*, an elderly farm labourer, saunters in.*	
BILLY	Mornin'.	10
PERCY	You'm late.	
BILLY	Come day, go day, God send Sunday, if ever I come through theseyer door of a morning and your old watch bain't five minutes fast then the natural world as we knows it will have come to an end.	
PERCY	You'm late! Now. You'll be fencing up at the Far Hanging today. Take the Scotch cart an' all the things you need. Eph, I want you to go up to the lambing pen and give Tom a hand. He's been a bit busy at the moment, one way or another.	
BILLY	I never heerd tell o' such a thing. Boy-child, missus says. 'Poor little bastard,' I says to her.	20
	'Billy!' she says, 'your language!'	
	'That's what he is,' I says, 'a bastard, no messin'.' What do you reckon, Percy? Tom and Kathie be let keep un?	
PERCY	Depends. The mother might come back, I s'pose.	

4

EPHRAIM	Never.
BILLY	Does Mrs Yorke know?
PERCY	Yes. If Tom and Kathie decide to adopt the babbie, good luck to 'em, she said.
BILLY	What they going to call him?
PERCY	I got no idea, but I know what I'm going to call you if you don't get to work. Go on …

He watches them go, rubbing his knee.

STORYTELLER	Percy Pound, the farm foreman. German shell fragment smashed that knee in the Battle of the Somme, 1916. Ten years ago now.

***Percy** limps to the Sparrows' cottage door and knocks with his stick. **Kathie** answers, carrying the baby.*

PERCY	Morning, Kath. How's it going then? Anything we can do to help?
KATHIE	It's alright thanks, Percy.

***Percy** looks at the baby.*

STORYTELLER	'No beauty,' he thought.
KATHIE	He's beautiful, isn't he?
PERCY	What you going to call him then?
KATHIE	Well, Tom wants to call him John after his old dad and I want to call him Joe after mine.
PERCY	You'll have to toss for it then.
KATHIE	Don't know as we'll be let keep him. After all, tisn't as though he's a normal baby.
PERCY	Not normal? What do you mean?
KATHIE	I mean, we don't know who he belongs to.

30

40

50

3 ❖ SPIDER

Forwards in time now. The Sparrows' cottage garden. A two-and-a-half year-old child **1**
scuttles round on all fours in an unusual manner, keeping his knees up off the ground,
playing with a ball. **Kathie** *takes in some washing.* **Tom** *hoes his cabbage patch.*

STORYTELLER	John Joseph Sparrow …
STORYTELLER	… rather more than two years later, and still no signs of him walking.
STORYTELLER	But he got about smartly enough.
STORYTELLER	Kathie and Tom had finally been able to adopt him.

Tom *tickles* **Spider** *and he squirms with delight.*

KATHIE	Spider!	**10**

STORYTELLER — Everyone called him that now, because of his peculiar way of crawling.

Spider *crawls to* **Kathie***'s feet.*

KATHIE — Who's a good boy?

He prods himself in the chest.

SPIDER — Good un!

STORYTELLER — At almost two-and-a-half, that's all he said.

STORYTELLER — Tom and Kath both worried.

KATHIE — It's time for his bed. Say goodnight to your dad, Spider.

SPIDER	Good un!	**20**

KATHIE — You and your 'good un'. Say good *night*, there's a good boy.

SPIDER — Good un!

TOM — Sleep well, my son.

KATHIE	Goodnight, my love.
TOM	Pleasant dreams.
	Kathie tucks Spider into his cot and he falls asleep almost immediately. She creeps away.
KATHIE	I suppose he does dream. He sleeps so sound. I don't think he's ever woke us.
TOM	He's contented, that's why. 30
	Tom gets into bed and Kathie joins him. Tom soon begins to snore, but Kathie lies awake. Outside, an owl hoots.
STORYTELLER	It was some time in the small hours when Kath heard that old owl, out on his usual perch in the apple tree at the bottom of the garden.
	Unseen by Kathie, Spider sits up in his cot and hoots loudly in a perfect imitation of the owl, then lies down again. Kathie sits up sharply and creeps to Spider's cot. He's fast asleep again. Kathie returns to bed and sits.
KATHIE	Must've dreamt it. 40
	Morning comes. Tom gets up with a stretch and a yawn, splashes water on his face and puts on his hat. Kathie gets Spider out of his cot, and he babbles happily.
SPIDER	Good un …
KATHIE	Bye dear.
	Tom kisses her and pinches Spider's cheek, copying his babble.
SPIDER	Good un.
TOM	Good un! Come on, Molly.
MOLLY	Woof!
	Tom goes off for the day. Spider plays happily in the garden 50 while Kathie puts more washing out.

STORYTELLER	Not long after Tom left, a cuckoo flew across the nearby field.
CUCKOO	Cuckoo. Cuckoo.
SPIDER	Cuckoo! Cuckoo!
KATHIE	Spider! It *was* you last night then!
SPIDER	Good un!
KATHIE	There's clever you are! Maybe I'm wrong. Maybe you'll be cleverer than the other children …

*Kathie goes back to her washing. A **cat** jumps up on the garden wall.*   60

STORYTELLER	The Sparrows' neighbours had a big old ginger tom that sometimes paid a visit.
CAT	Miaow.
SPIDER	Miaow!

*The **cat** looks at **Spider**, rather surprised.*

CAT	Miaow.

*Kathie watches, transfixed. Suddenly the **cat** jumps down and runs towards **Spider**.*

KATHIE	Spider!

*Kathie rushes to save him but finds the **cat** nuzzling his face,*   70
purring loudly.

Spider?

*The **cat** runs away. **Kathie** picks **Spider** up, who purrs loudly. She kisses him and puts him back in his cot. **Tom** comes home.*

KATHIE	… I couldn't believe my ears. He had all those different sounds exactly.
TOM	Well I never. And he weren't frightened of that old cat then?
KATHIE	No!

TOM	Just as well he is fond of animals if he's going to work on the farm.	80
KATHIE	He might not, you never know, he might learn a trade, go to work in town perhaps …	

Tom decides the moment has come to talk openly.

TOM	Kath, love, let's be straight with one another, we always have. He's slow, our Spider, isn't he now?	
KATHIE	He'll catch up. Look how clever he is making all those noises … oh, Tom …	
TOM	We ought to look on the bright side. He's healthy and he's happy.	
KATHIE	You never know, we might be wrong! No one in the village has said anything to me. Have the farm men said anything to you?	90
TOM	No …	

Percy Pound, Billy Butt and Ephraim gather in the stable for the day's orders. Ephraim brushes a horse. Billy goes on, as usual.

BILLY	… Same as I told the missus, Tom and Kathie'd been better off without un. Why, if that had been a lamb as wasn't right, Tom would have knocked 'ee on the head, thee'st know. I bain't sayin' he shoulda done that to the babbie, but he ought to have let un fade away.	100
EPHRAIM	Not for my money, Billy. I reckon Tom done right.	
PERCY	*(Angrily.)* And so do I. And I'm telling you two, you keep your mouths shut about that kid. If I hear anyone's been poking fun so Kath and Tom gets to hear of it, you'll get your cards, understand?	
BILLY/EPHRAIM	*(Muttering.)* Ar.	

Each goes off to their day's work.

4 ❖ SCHOOL

STORYTELLER	The years passed and it was lambing time again on Outoverdown Farm.	1

Kathie walks along a country lane. She turns back and beckons.

KATHIE   Spider! Come on. We'll be late.

Spider stumps along, joyfully soaking up the world around him. He walks upright now but with a peculiar lolloping gait.

STORYTELLER   It was also John Joseph Sparrow's sixth birthday, so quickly does time fly.

Kathie neatens his hair fondly. A flock of lapwings lifts out of a nearby field with mournful cries.   **10**

SPIDER   Peewit! Peewit!

KATHIE   That's right!

Spider points at himself.

SPIDER   Good un!

KATHIE   Yes.

*A grand old country lady, **Mrs Yorke**, comes on horseback down the lane towards them now.*

SPIDER   Missus!

STORYTELLER   Mrs Yorke, the owner of Outoverdown. She'd run the farm alone since her husband died in the Great War.   **20**

MRS YORKE   Good morning, Mrs Sparrow!

KATHIE   Morning, ma'am.

MRS YORKE   And young Master Sparrow! At last we meet!

Spider hides behind his mum.

KATHIE	It's his birthday, ma'am.
MRS YORKE	Tell me, young man, how old are you now?
KATHIE	Spider, show Mrs Yorke how old you are.

Spider shyly holds up the fingers and thumb of one hand.

That's five, love. That's what you were yesterday. Today   30
you're six. Remember?

Kathie holds up six fingers. *Spider* copies and looks at his
fingers and thumbs as if they don't belong to him. *Kathie*
speaks to *Mrs Yorke*.

We're off up to the school to see Mr Pugh about him
starting …

Mrs Yorke can't help but watch *Spider*. It's dawning on her
that he's different to other children. *Spider* hops about with
excitement and points over a wall.

SPIDER	Barrits!	40
KATHIE	Yes, rabbits! *(To **Mrs Yorke**.)* He loves animals. They seem to love him too.	
MRS YORKE	No wonder.	
KATHIE	We best be off. Mustn't be late for Mr Pugh.	
MRS YORKE	Quite! Well, the best of British luck.	
KATHIE	Spider, come along. Say goodbye to Mrs Yorke.	
SPIDER	Spider six!	
MRS YORKE	So you are! Cheerio, my boy.	

Kathie and *Spider* walk on their way. *Mrs Yorke* watches
for a while.   50

CROWS	Caw! Caw!
SPIDER	Croaks!

KATHIE	Crows, yes. How many?
SPIDER	Six?
KATHIE	No. Count them. Use your fingers.
	Spider lags behind, trying to count with his fingers. Kathie passes three boys about Spider's age.
PHILLIP	Hello, Mrs Sparrow.
KATHIE	Hello, Phillip.
	Spider passes them. Suddenly they make a cruel impersonation 60 of Spider's voice.
BOY 1	Hullo, Spider.
BOY 2	Good un!
	Spider hurries to catch up with his mother. The Boys follow, copying his walk.
BOYS	Good un! Good un!
	Kathie turns round and they stop copying.
KATHIE	Spider!
	Kathie looks at them knowingly, then takes Spider by the hand and turns in at the school gate. 70
BOY 3	Spider! Ee'd have frightened Miss Muffet to death, 'ee would!
	Spider looks overawed as Kathie pulls him across the playground full of shouting children and into the schoolhouse. Mr Pugh sits marking. Kathie and Spider stand unnoticed for a moment before Mr Pugh comes round his desk to greet them.
MR PUGH	Mrs Sparrow, and this must be John Joseph … *(He shakes their hands.)* Please, take a seat. I've heard such a lot about you, John. It's a pleasure to meet you at last.
KATHIE	Say hello, Spider. *(He can't say a word.)* Spider's what we call him at home. 80

MR PUGH	I see. Now the vicar has told me something of his condition, but you'll understand, I wanted to meet him myself, to ascertain whether he'll fit in with us or not.
KATHIE	Yes.
MR PUGH	I'll ask him some questions, if I may …
KATHIE	Please.
MR PUGH	Now then, young man. Let's see how much you know.

Mr Pugh writes CAT in big letters on a slate and holds it up.

What does that say?

No answer. He writes the letter A.   90

Well, what does that letter say?

Nothing. He writes the letter B.

How about that one?

Spider looks at *Kathie* as if to say, 'Take me away.'

No? Never mind. Let me see …

Mr Pugh opens an illustrated encyclopedia and shows *Spider* a picture of a huge ship being launched.

What do you see here? What's going on?

He flicks to another picture, this time of a man working on an early car production line.   100

What's he doing?

Still Spider is unable to reply. Mr Pugh turns the pages and finds a picture of a rabbit.

What's that?

SPIDER	*(Very quietly.)* Barrit.
MR PUGH	Can he write his name, Mrs Sparrow?

KATHIE	No.
MR PUGH	Does he know any numbers?
KATHIE	He knows how old he is.
MR PUGH	How old are you, John? Spider? 110

Spider is confused and holds up only five fingers.

KATHIE	He's just six …

*There's a moment's pause while **Mr Pugh** chooses his words.*

He's ever so clever in some ways! He's wonderful with animals, any sort of animal, and he can copy the noises they make to the life …

MR PUGH	Mrs Sparrow, it's better if I'm frank with you. Your boy has got problems that I don't think we can deal with. I'm sorry.

*Mr Pugh leaves them. **Kathie** sits with her head in her hands.*

SPIDER	Mum? Spider not go school? 120

She shakes her head.

Good un!

*Spider looks so happy **Kathie** can't help but laugh and hug him.*

5 ❖ ANIMALS

Mrs Yorke and Percy stroll into a field of cows that are mooing contentedly. 1

MRS YORKE   A nice bunch these, Percy.

PERCY   Bull's done his job, any road.

MRS YORKE   I've been meaning to ask you, Percy – you remember a few years back when Tom and Kathie Sparrow took on that abandoned baby?

PERCY   Course, ma'am.

MRS YORKE   Well I've just seen the child and he's half-witted, no doubt about it.

PERCY   That's right.   10

MRS YORKE   Am I the last person in the valley to know?

PERCY   Maybe there's a few o' those heifers as don't know yet …

MRS YORKE   Damn bad luck on the Sparrows.

PERCY   Ar. Sweet lad, though.

MRS YORKE   Yes. Very. Perhaps we could find him something to do on the farm when he's older, something simple.

PERCY   If you say so, ma'am.

MRS YORKE   Yes, I think I do, Percy! *(They exit.)*

Kathie is dressed for cleaning. She brings Spider into the garden and sits him down with a tin of shoe polish, a brush and   20 some shoes, and shows him how to clean them.

KATHIE   Think you can manage that?

SPIDER   Yes, Mum.

KATHIE   I'm at the front cleaning windows if you want me. And try and keep the polish off your trousers.

Spider starts to apply the polish liberally.

SPIDER   Yes, Mum.

Kathie slips some newspaper onto his lap, under the boot, and goes off to clean windows.

STORYTELLER   Spider was ten now and Kathie didn't keep as sharp an eye   30
on him as she used to.

Three schoolboys creep up outside the garden wall. They giggle and pull brown sacks over their heads, roughly drawn with the faces of dogs. One of them peeps round the wall and barks once at *Spider* then ducks out of sight. *Spider* looks over. The *boy* barks again.

SPIDER   Mum? Dog's barking …

Spider goes to investigate but the *three boys* circle behind him to block his route back to his house. One of the boys barks again. *Spider* turns and sees them. He goes to run past them   40
but they fan out to stop him.

Mum? Mum!

The *boys* start to growl viciously. *Spider* backs away. Suddenly one of them barks loudly. *Spider* cries out with fear. They all start barking. *Spider* runs away.

BOY 1   Come on … get after 'im!

BOY 2   Tally ho!

BOY 3   Tally ho!

*They run after *Spider* like a pack of hounds.*

KATHIE   Have you finished, love? Spider? 'Cause I've got your   50
father's for you to do, too …

Kathie comes into the garden but finds *Spider* gone.

Spider …? Spider?

She fetches her hat and coat and sets off to look for him.

16

Spider runs into a field and falls exhausted. The **boys** encircle him, baying wildly.

SPIDER   Want go home please.

Boy 1 pushes *Spider* over from behind. He gets up. **Boy 2** pushes him over. He gets up again and **Boy 3** pushes him over. *Spider* doesn't get up this time. The **boys** close in on him now, pretending   60
to be hounds, tearing at him, ripping his clothes. *Spider* cries.

BOY 1   'Ere! Cowpat!

They drag **Spider** *over and push his face into it.*

'Ow's that then? Good un!

BOYS 2/3   Good un! Good un!

Spider stumbles about, unable to see properly. **Boy 1** fetches a stick to hit him with but **Boy 2** stops him.

BOY 2   What you doing?

BOY 1   Gonna whack 'im!

BOY 3   Don't be daft.   70

BOY 2   Nobody said anything about whackin' 'im …

BOY 1   Where is 'ee?

Spider has escaped. The **boys** take off their masks.

BOY 2   I'm going 'ome.

BOY 3   Me too.

BOY 1   Chickens! … Chickens!

He smacks the ground with his stick and runs off home too, throwing his mask over a hedge.

Kathie comes home. She calls one last time at the back door.

KATHIE   Spider! It's teatime. Where are you?   80

17

She goes inside and sits to think. Suddenly she hears a little noise from under the kitchen table.

Spider? Is that you?

She crouches and sees him hiding there.

What's the matter? It's alright, dear.

Spider *crawls out and kneels, shivering.*

Good God ... what happened?

SPIDER	Sorry, Mum, sorry. Bad boys. Bad boys.
KATHIE	Boys did this? Spider? Boys hurt you?
SPIDER	Bad boys.
KATHIE	Who did this? Who?

90

Kathie runs to the back door and screams with all her heart.

ANIMALS!

She hugs **Spider** *and weeps.* **Tom** *comes in from work now. With one look he seems to understand what's happened, almost to have anticipated it. He puts his arms round his family.*

6 ❖ CROWSTARVING

STORYTELLER	Three years later, on the third of September 1939, Britain was forced once more to declare war on Germany. The only sons of both Mrs Yorke and Percy enlisted within the first few weeks.
	***Percy** and **Mrs Yorke** have come to look at a field of winter wheat.*
MRS YORKE	Damn crows … to Hell with you!
CROWS	Caw! Caw!
MRS YORKE	This is War Wheat! Whose side are you on …?
	I wonder what they'll call this one?
PERCY	Beg pardon, ma'am?
MRS YORKE	This war. If the last was the 'Great' War, what's this one?
PERCY	The next war, I s'pose. What's your boy signed up for, ma'am?
MRS YORKE	The air force. Yours?
PERCY	Wiltshires.
MRS YORKE	Must we give our sons? When we've already given so much? Sorry, Percy.
PERCY	Poor young Albie Stanhope.
MRS YORKE	Ephraim's boy?
PERCY	Yes. 'Ee joined the yeomanry for the horses and they went over to tanks the following week … *(They laugh. He shouts at the crows.)* Clear off!
CROWS	Caw! Caw!

1

10

20

19

MRS YORKE	It's no good, Percy. If this wheat's to stand a chance, it needs someone to look after it.
PERCY	We're a bit shorthanded without Albie, ma'am.
MRS YORKE	How old's the Sparrows' boy now?
PERCY	Spider? Thirteen, I reckon. Maybe a bit more.
MRS YORKE	Strong lad, is he?
PERCY	Well, he don't carry much flesh.
MRS YORKE	But it wouldn't be hard work, would it?
PERCY	I'll ask Tom, ma'am …

30

Mrs Yorke goes off. *Tom* approaches.

TOM	Crowstarvin'?
PERCY	He could do that, couldn't he? Make a noise, shout and yell, bang on a bit of tin, keep the birds away?

Tom thinks. *Percy* goes off. *Kathie* approaches.

KATHIE	Crowstarving? That's not much of a job, out in all weathers. He'll catch his death of cold and he'll be all on his own.
TOM	He likes being on his own, Kath, you know that. He can't come to no harm, so long as you wrap him up warm.
KATHIE	But crowstarving … he won't ever do that. He loves the birds.

40

Kathie goes off. *Spider* approaches.

TOM	Spider? How'd you like to work on the farm, like Dada does?
SPIDER	Sheep?
TOM	No. Looking after the corn. Your job'd be to frighten the birds away.
SPIDER	Spider frighten birds?

50

TOM	Yes.
SPIDER	Sparrows?
TOM	No.
SPIDER	Birdblacks?
TOM	No. Croaks.
SPIDER	Spider frighten croaks?
TOM	You remember when those boys pushed you over? In the cow muck?
SPIDER	Bad boys.
TOM	Yes. Well now, the croaks are bad birds, stealing Mrs's corn. You're going to be a kind of a sojer, like Albie. He's gone to fight the Germans, you've got to frighten the croaks.

Spider gets excited, hopping from foot to foot, swinging his arms.

SPIDER	Spider sojer?
TOM	*(Nods.)* What d'you think?
SPIDER	Good un!

60

7 ❖ FRIENDS

*It's **Spider's** first day of work. Before he leaves home, **Kathie** dresses him in **Tom's** old army greatcoat that comes down to his ankles and pulls a thick balaclava over his head.*

KATHIE	Arms out … arms down … this'll keep you warm.
	Lunch.
	*Kathie puts a packet of sandwiches in **Spider**'s pocket then she kisses him goodbye and he sets off with **Tom**. When **Kathie**'s out of sight, **Tom** takes the balaclava off **Spider**.*
TOM	Now. I got to go on up to see the lambs. Find Percy. He'll tell you what to do.
	Spider looks a bit nervous.
	You just do as you're told and you won't come to no harm.
SPIDER	Bye Dada.
TOM	Have a good day, my boy … go on! Come on, Molly.
	Spider walks alone into the stables down at Outoverdown Farm.
EPHRAIM	Hello Spider. What you doing here?
SPIDER	Croaks! Bad croaks!
	He flaps his arms.
EPHRAIM	Right you are.
	*Spider goes up to **Flower**, the cart horse, in her stall.*
	You want to be careful, Spider. Old Flower, she don't like kids near her as a rule.
SPIDER	Spider like horses.

10

20

EPHRAIM	Well, don't say I didn't warn you.
	Spider pats *Flower*, *mumbling to her gently. The horse seems to enjoy the attention.*
	Well, I never …
	Percy comes in.
PERCY	Morning, Eph.
EPHRAIM	Morning, Percy.
PERCY	Tom Sparrow's boy's starting today, crowstarving up at Mag's Corner.
EPHRAIM	That what he's on about.
PERCY	Here already, is he?
EPHRAIM	Ar, and I'll tell you something for nothing, he's either fearless or foolish.
	Ephraim points at Spider, who's leant against Flower, whispering in her ear. Percy leans on Flower's rump in his habitual position and looks at his watch with a shake of his head. Billy comes in.
BILLY	Yur, 'tis brass monkey weather out there. I 'opes you got a nice warm job for me today, Percy, I ain't so young as I was …
	Spider has been stood at Flower's head, out of sight. Now he comes and copies Percy, throwing an arm casually over her rump. Flower is quite unbothered. Billy, for once, is lost for words.
PERCY	This is Tom and Kathie's boy. He's starting work today. Now I don't want anyone poking fun at him 'cause he doesn't speak too well. Spider, tell 'em what you're going to do today.
SPIDER	Spider scare croaks!

30

40

50

*The **Farm men** go off to work. **Percy** loads **Spider** up with a big bit of old tin and a metal bar, then throws his stiff leg over his motorbike and starts it up. He pats the pillion seat.*

PERCY   Come on, Spider.

***Spider** climbs on in a state of disbelief.*

Hold tight!

*They roar up the rough farm road, **Spider** yelling with excitement, until they come to a huge field high on the Downs. **Percy** leads them creeping through the gate. Once inside, they can hear hundreds of crows happily feasting in the field.*   60

Quiet … now then, sojer, see all the bad birds down there, stealing Mrs Yorke's corn? (***Spider** nods.*) Right then, up and at 'em!

***Spider** looks at the tin and bar, then at **Percy**, then at the crows before marching into the field, banging his piece of tin for all he's worth.*

SPIDER   Gedoff croaks! Bad croaks! Bad uns! Bad uns!

***Spider** crashes round joyfully, totally free. **Percy** leaves him to it and rides off on his motorbike. When **Spider** has finished, he sits down to eat his lunch.*   70

STORYTELLER   Crowstarving was the ideal job for Spider. All around him were animals of one sort or another.

PIGEONS   Coo-coo-roo, coo-coo …

***Spider** replies.*

SPIDER   Coo-coo-roo, coo-coo. Pigeons.

Suddenly all the pigeons lift off at once.

Pigeons scared.

***Spider** is transfixed. A **fox** is standing there. Very warily it creeps closer and sits. **Spider** breaks off a bit of his sandwich and holds it out, speaking softly.*   80

Good un.

*Slowly, slowly the **fox** approaches, until it takes the food right from **Spider's** hand. It backs a few feet then delicately eats the bread. When it has finished it looks at **Spider** a moment more, then trots away.*

STORYTELLER The fox came again the next day and the next day and the day after that to share his bit of bread and cheese. They became friends of sorts, Spider and that fox. 90

*It starts to rain. **Spider** looks at the sky, then at his coat as it soaks up the rain thirstily.*

8 ❖ Losses

Spider comes home. Kathie peels his soaking coat off him. Spider fetches a 1
children's encyclopedia of animals while Kathie and Tom talk.

KATHIE	If it's weather like this tomorrow then he's not going out, and you can tell Percy I said so.
	Spider finds a portrait of a fox and shows them excitedly.
SPIDER	Spider see!
TOM	Saw a fox did you?
SPIDER	Vox! Vox! Good un!
	He points at his mouth and makes a chewing movement.
TOM	Eating summat, was it?
SPIDER	Spider eat, vox eat.
	He mimes breaking off some bread and offering it to the fox.
TOM	Shared your lunch with a fox!
	Spider nods vigorously.
KATHIE	Honestly! Don't know what goes on inside his head sometimes!
TOM	Dunno what Mrs Yorke'd say! Only good fox for her is a dead one!
	Kathie shushes him and points at Spider.
KATHIE	Anyway. He'll catch his death, standing about with nowhere to shelter.
TOM	All right, all right, I'll fix something up for him.
STORYTELLER	The next morning, Tom and Ephraim made a shelter for Spider.

10

20

*For a finishing touch, **Tom** puts a crate inside for a seat. **Molly** runs into the shelter.*

TOM   Molly! There. Spider?

SPIDER   Spider's house?

TOM   That's right! Show us what you're going to do then, if it's raining.   30

Spider ducks in, sits on the crate and beams at the two of them. They know just what he's going to say.

SPIDER/TOM/   Good un!
EPHRAIM

*Spider shuts the 'door' to test out his shelter. **Tom** and **Ephraim** hear a **pack of hounds** in full cry in the distance.*

MOLLY   Woof!

TOM   Shush, Molly! Mrs Yorke'll be out with the hunt then.

EPHRAIM   Oh ar – riding over someone else's land today. Mrs Yorke don't want 'em trampin' all over her precious corn.   40

Suddenly the noise stops.

TOM   Sounds like they got their fox, then. See you teatime, Spider.

Spider sticks his head out of the flap.

SPIDER   Bye Dada!

TOM   Come on, Molly.

EPHRAIM   See you, Spider.

SPIDER   Bye Eph.

*Tom and **Ephraim** go, taking **Molly** with them. **Spider** gets out his sandwiches.*

STORYTELLER Spider waited for his fox to come and claim a share again.   50
                 But he couldn't possibly know that the cry of the pack had

stopped so suddenly because the hounds had caught and killed his friend.

Percy is shuffling past his front door in his shirtsleeves and slippers with a tray of tea when a letter falls through his letterbox.

STORYTELLER   On the tenth of June 1940, Percy Pound and his wife received a telegram from the War Office.

Percy knows what it is the moment he sees it. Reluctantly, he picks it up and reads it.   60

STORYTELLER   It regretted to inform them that their only son had been killed in action during the retreat from Dunkirk.

Tom, Mrs Yorke and Kathie stand in a line to offer their mumbled condolences. Percy walks past them in a daze, nodding in acknowledgement but without being able to look at them. Spider is the last in line and smiles warmly, not appreciating the gravity of the situation.

SPIDER   Morning, Percy!

PERCY   Morning, Spider.

9 ❖ HARVEST

STORYTELLER	Harvest time came, same as every year.	1

*The **Farmworkers** bring sheaves of wheat to a wagon and load them on. **Spider** arrives and immediately gets in **Ephraim's** way.*

PERCY   Want to do something really helpful?

***Spider** nods eagerly.*

Right then. Go down to the farm and get me a ball o' binder twine from the stable. *(To the other men.)* Well, come on you rabble, let's get this lot on the wagon.

***Spider** sets off. The men work in silence, lifting the sheaves up with forks and stacking them up high on the cart.*   10

STORYTELLER   It was a traditional English country scene as peaceful as could be …

Suddenly, two aeroplanes approach fast and low, one firing on the other.

EPHRAIM   Fighters!

BILLY   Oo's chasin' 'oo?

EPHRAIM   I can't see …

The planes pass close overhead.

He's hit a German!   20

BILLY   One of our boys?

EPHRAIM   Yes!

EPHRAIM/BILLY   Hooray!

BILLY   Hit a German?

PERCY	Yes. He's going down near the farm.
EPHRAIM	Come on! Let's get him!
PERCY	Steady. Be quicker on the tractor.

Percy, *Billy* and *Ephraim* set off. Meanwhile, down the hill, *Spider* ambles along in a world of his own.

STORYTELLER	Spider was half way down to the farm when he heard the planes. He saw one high above, twisting itself in a victory roll. Then he saw another coming over the shoulder of the hill quite silently, for its engine was dead. It was sweeping straight towards him …	30

*The plane passes just over **Spider**'s head with a great whoosh, knocking him flat before skidding to a halt on its belly behind him. **Spider** picks himself up and watches the **Pilot** jump out of the plane unhurt. When the **Pilot** hears voices and the tractor approaching, he runs away. **Billy** can be heard already, shouting in high excitement. He arrives with a pitchfork in his hands.*   40

BILLY	… if so be 'ee's alive, old Billy'll soon put that right. Stick un right through his German guts, I shall … there! Lookzee, the bagger's alive! I'm going to stick this yer pick in thy arse!
EPHRAIM	Bide quiet, Billy. That's our Spider.
BILLY	Where be the pilot then?
PERCY	Dead in the cockpit maybe. No … it's empty.
BILLY	Where is he then, Spider? Didst see un? Where's he to?
PERCY	Steady, Billy. Spider, did you see the man?

Spider nods.   50

Where'd he go?

SPIDER	Spider's house.
BILLY	Come on then!

| PERCY | Wait. He may be armed. It's no good rushing in there, mad headed. Keep behind me. |

*They surround **Spider**'s house. **Percy** stands opposite the entrance with the pitchfork poised.*

Eph, you go round the back in case he breaks that way. Take Billy with you. Come on, Spider.

*They fan out quietly. When everyone is in place, **Percy** shouts.*   60

Come out with your hands up ...! Hande hoch ...! Come out, you murdering swine!

*Hesitantly, the **German pilot** comes out of the shelter with his hands up.*

| PILOT | Ich ergebe mich, Kamerad ... bitte ... tun Sie mir nichts ... |

***Percy** slowly lowers the pitchfork.*

| PERCY | Dear God ... he looks just like my son ... |

| SPIDER | Good un. |

***Percy**, **Billy**, **Ephraim** and **Spider** escort their prisoner away.*   70

10 ❖ Only a Watch

STORYTELLER	The German pilot was taken off that same afternoon to a prisoner-of-war camp near Salisbury. Once the wreckage was cleared away, all that remained of the crash was a scar on the grass where the plane had slithered to a halt. Life soon went on as best it could on Outoverdown Farm, in spite of the war.	1

Spider wanders up and looks over the wall of a bridge at the river flowing under it, then sits up on the parapet, clumsily swinging his legs over.

STORYTELLER	Spider often walked by the river in his spare time. One Sunday he'd glimpsed an otter by the bridge and now he came back at the same time every Sunday in the hope of seeing another.	10

Spider gets a watch out of his pocket and checks the time.

Tom and Kathie had given him a wrist-watch for his fourteenth birthday, which he insisted on carrying in his pocket for safety, or so he thought …

*Suddenly, and violently, **Spider** sneezes. The watch drops into the water. He leans out over the parapet to see where it has gone, loses his balance and falls in after it. He goes under for a moment, then bobs to the surface, screaming. **Percy** appears on the riverbank.* 20

PERCY	Spider? Dear God … I'm coming, boy!

Spider goes under.

Spider!

Spider bobs up again, weaker now, his last breath not far off. *Percy* wades into the river and holds out his walking stick.

Catch hold of this.

Spider just manages to reach it.

That's it! Hold on, Spider, hold on tight!

Awkwardly, **Percy** *drags him out onto the bank where he coughs*   30
and gasps, eyes wide in terror. **Percy** *holds him and rocks him.*

You're alright now … That's right, you cough it up. Better
out than in, eh?!

STORYTELLER Somehow, he got Spider home.

Tom *and* **Kathie** *rush to* **Percy***, and* **Tom** *takes hold of*
Spider*.* **Kathie** *embraces* **Percy** *in an uncharacteristic display*
of affection.

KATHIE Oh, Percy … how grateful we are to you.

TOM We are.

PERCY Poor lad. Once he got his voice back, all he could say was   40
'watch'. He must've dropped it in.

TOM It's only a watch. We've still got our son …

Tom *realises what he's said, to* **Percy** *of all people.*

PERCY It's alright, Tom. It's alright.

Percy *ruffles* **Spider***'s hair then takes his leave of the*
Sparrows.

On his way home he meets **Mrs Yorke***, lost in thought with a*
telegram of her own in her hands.

PERCY Mrs Yorke.

MRS YORKE Oh … Percy.   50

PERCY Is it your boy, ma'am?

MRS YORKE He's alright, Percy. Crashed in France though. Been taken
prisoner, it seems. Could be worse, I suppose.

PERCY He's a strong lad. He can look after himself.

MRS YORKE	Yes. I wish I could speak to him though.
PERCY	Yes.

Mrs Yorke can't help crying now. ***Percy*** *gives her his handkerchief.*

MRS YORKE	Sorry, Percy.
PERCY	No, no. Not at all …

60

Percy *wants to offer some comfort but he's unsure what's appropriate between a man of his station and a lady, so he pats* ***Mrs Yorke****'s arm, for which she seems very grateful.*

MRS YORKE	Dear Percy. Thank you … have you been swimming?
PERCY	After a fashion, ma'am. Pulled young Spider out of the river.
MRS YORKE	What on earth was he doing?
PERCY	Dropped his watch off the bridge, it seems. Matter of fact, you can still see it, led in the bottom, clear as can be …
MRS YORKE	Perhaps we should get it out for him …?
PERCY	No point, ma'am. Works'll be all rusted up.

70

MRS YORKE	How sad.
PERCY	Yes. Gives a funny feelin', seein' it under the water, stopped forever at half past ten. Any road, best be off home. Lunch'll be on the table.
MRS YORKE	Yes. Better not keep Mrs Pound waiting.
PERCY	No! Take care, ma'am.
MRS YORKE	I shall. You too, Percy.

Percy *goes on home.*

11 ❖ A FINE CHALLENGE

Mrs Yorke sits in her favourite armchair to read her paper.   1

STORYTELLER   Above all things, Mrs Yorke loved horses. One day, a most
                 intriguing advertisement caught her eye …

MRS YORKE   'One American "Bronco" stallion to be sold at auction at
                 Salisbury Market …'

                 And so to the auction. **Mrs Yorke** *listens attentively to the auctioneer.*

AUCTIONEER   Lot 23, one American stallion. Tennenbaum's American
                 Travelling Show is selling up and going home, but they're
                 not going to the bother of shipping this fella back. He's a
                 'bucking bronco', which means they used him in their   10
                 rodeo show for young fools to fall off, so he's a bit wild but
                 a good, strong horse. George, let's 'ave a look at 'im.

                 There's a wild neighing and crashing out of sight, then the
                 bronco *drags* **George** *into the ring, rearing, bucking, turning,*
                 stamping, whinnying. **George** *clings to the halter as long as he*
                 can, then is thrown to the ground and runs for his life.

GEORGE   Mother!

                 The ***bronco*** *crashes back out of the ring. There's silence at the*
                 auction for a second or two.

AUCTIONEER   There you have it, ladies and gentlemen. A fine challenge   20
                 for someone. Who will start the bidding for me at one
                 guinea …? No? Ten shillings? Ten shillings? Five shillings …?
                 Come on, you lot. Must be a home somewhere for this
                 magnificent beast … shame to send him for cat meat …

MRS YORKE   I'll buy him!

                 The **Auctioneer** *taps his gavel very quickly.*

AUCTIONEER   Sold then, to Mrs Yorke. *(Under his breath.)* And the best of
                 luck to her …

STORYTELLER	When the haulier arrived at Outoverdown Farm with the horse, Mrs Yorke was waiting with Ephraim at the bottom of the drove.

30

MRS YORKE	*(To the **Haulier**.)* We're going to run him straight up onto our top pasture, let him blow off some steam for a while.
EPHRAIM	For you to ride, is 'ee ma'am?
MRS YORKE	I don't know if I'll be riding him, Ephraim. To tell you the truth, I felt sorry for him.

*The **bronco** bursts out of the van and thunders off up the drove.*

EPHRAIM	'Ee's a bucking bronco alright, ma'am.
MRS YORKE	Oh … he'll soon settle down.

*The **bronco** comes close and grazes quietly a moment.*
*__Mrs Yorke__ and **Ephraim** creep up with a halter.*

40

EPHRAIM	Good 'orse … good 'orse … good 'orse …

*Suddenly, the **bronco** rears and runs off like the wind.*

EPHRAIM	I suppose we could run 'im into a tight spot and we might be able to handle him.
MRS YORKE	Corral him, like the cowboys in the movies!
EPHRAIM	I wouldn't know about that, ma'am. Only bin to the pictures once in Warminster, and that were Charlie Chaplin. The lambing pens'd be the place to hold 'im.
STORYTELLER	Mrs Yorke planned the whole operation with military precision.

50

MRS YORKE	… Ephraim and I will drive him out of the Far Hanging on Em'ly and Jack. Billy will turn him down the drove, Tom and Percy will head him into the sheep pen at the bottom. All clear? Good luck!

*Everyone goes away after the **bronco**. All is quiet for a moment.*

*But now there's an approaching hullabaloo and the **bronco**
rushes into the sheep pen and circles, finding itself closed in by
Mrs Yorke and the **Farmworkers**. Finally it stops in a
corner, panting heavily, eyeing the humans with fear and fury.
They too are breathing hard from the chase.*   60

MRS YORKE   Right, let's get a halter on him and we can tie him up.

             No one comes forward.

BILLY   Begging your pardon, ma'am, when I were a young chap I
             might have, but I bain't so quick on me feet as I was …

MRS YORKE   Come on, come on …

BILLY   I don't want to make our Martha a widder, ma'am.

EPHRAIM   Save thy breath, Billy. This here's my job.

             ***Ephraim** advances gingerly on the horse with a halter.*

             Good 'orse … good 'orse … good 'orse …

             *Suddenly the **bronco** erupts, bucking and neighing. **Ephraim**   70
             is knocked to the ground, and lies in danger of being trampled.
             Spider enters the enclosure and walks fearlessly towards the
             bronco, which calms down immediately. **Ephraim** scrambles
             for safety.*

BILLY   Spider …!

             ***Spider** snickers softly to the **bronco**. It snickers back, still
             edgy. Gently, **Spider** brings his hand up to the **bronco**'s face.
             It sniffs **Spider** and he strokes its nose.*

SPIDER   Good un. Good un.

             *The **bronco** tosses its head amicably with a gentle neigh.*   80

BILLY   Well … that's summint y'don't see every day.

12 ❖ THE REWARD

STORYTELLER	So began quite a new routine for the crowstarver.	1

*Spider goes into the pen with the **bronco**, holding a rope halter at his side. He talks to it and makes comfortable horse noises. He also strokes and pats it.*

STORYTELLER He always carried a rope halter, which he showed to the horse.

*He lets the **bronco** see and sniff the halter and lays it against his neck.*

STORYTELLER	Until the day came when he was able to slip it over his head.	10

*Spider leads the horse round and round. **Ephraim** slips into the pen and they try to swap.*

STORYTELLER At first he would only tolerate Ephraim if accompanied by Spider …

*The **bronco** kicks up until **Spider** comes back and talks to it, patting **Ephraim** like he was another horse.*

SPIDER Good un.

STORYTELLER Before long, it became clear the wild horse was wild no longer.

*Ephraim leads the **bronco** round. **Tom** brings **Spider** to Mrs Yorke in the stables. **Kathie** is waiting there too.*		20

MRS YORKE Spider, I wanted to thank you for all the wonderful work you've done with that bronco.

*She opens a door and four droop-eared, long-tailed **puppies** scurry in.*

Which one do you fancy, Spider? Take your pick.

SPIDER	Four puppies ...?	
TOM	One of them is for you.	
SPIDER	For Spider?	
TOM/MRS YORKE	Yes!	30
TOM	Which one do you want?	

*One of the dogs sits at **Spider**'s feet, yapping and wagging her tail. **Spider** picks her up and rubs his cheek against her head. He's in love.*

	Spider?	
SPIDER	Ta Missus!	
MRS YORKE	Quite alright, old chap.	

*She leaves them with the puppy **Spider** has chosen.*

TOM	What are we going to call her, then?	
KATHIE	Let Spider choose.	40
TOM	We'll have to help him. Spider, puppy's got to have a name. *(To Kathie.)* You start.	
KATHIE	How about ... Bess?	

***Spider** shakes his head.*

TOM	Nell?	

***Spider** shakes his head.*

KATHIE	Lady?	

***Spider** shakes his head.*

TOM	Princess?	

***Spider** shakes his head.* 50

KATHIE	Gracie?	

***Spider** shakes his head.*

TOM	Bonnie?
	Spider shakes his head.
KATHIE	Well, what d'you want to call her, Spider?
SPIDER	Missus!
	Kath and Tom look at each other.
KATHIE	That's nice, love, but you can't call her Missus.
TOM	How about … Sissie?
SPIDER	Sis-sie! Good un! Sis-sie!
	Spider goes off happily with the puppy.
KATHIE	Sissie?!
TOM	Don't worry. It'll soon shorten. I'll see to that.

60

13 ❖ T̲HE̲ H̲ARE̲

Spider runs into a field with his crowstarving piece of tin to bash.   1

SPIDER   Sis! Come!

STORYTELLER   The summer of 1941 was, for Spider, the happiest time of
                      his life so far.

SPIDER   Good Sis! Where's stick? Find stick!

                      Sis runs off to find a stick.

STORYTELLER   His happiness was almost wholly due to Sis.

                      *Sis comes back with a stick in her mouth and **Spider** uses it
                      to bang on his tin. **Sis** barks and runs in a wide circle, chasing
                      crows.*   10

SPIDER   Sorry croaks.

                      *Spider sits for a rest. **Sis** is a long way off now. As **Spider**
                      watches her, a large **hare** lollops just in front of him and lies in
                      the grass. **Spider** crouches and looks at it, mesmerised.*

                      Big barrit.

                      *Scenting **Spider** now, the **hare** begins to lope away. **Spider**
                      stands and watches the **hare** go out of sight, then, to his horror,
                      he sees **Sis** running towards it in the distance.*

                      No! Sis, no!

                      *Moments later, **Sis** runs up with the dead hare. She drops it in   20
                      front of **Spider**, looking to him for approval. **Spider** takes up
                      the hare and strokes it tenderly. It has been coming on darker for
                      a while. There's a rumble of thunder and the heavens open.
                      Spider carries the hare home in his arms. **Sis** follows close all
                      the way, confused by her master's behaviour. By the time they get
                      home, **Spider** and **Sis** are soaked and shivering. They come in
                      to the cottage kitchen. **Kathie** is cooking.*

| KATHIE | Spider, you must be soaked to the skin … |

Spider puts the dead hare on the kitchen table then lays his head on his arms and weeps. *Sis* lies next to him, tilting her head, puzzled by the crying. *Kathie* turns and sees the *hare*.   30

Oh, love.

Kathie strokes *Spider*'s hair then takes off his coat and fetches a towel to dry his head. *Tom* comes in from work.

| TOM | Gwor. Coming down stair rods out there … what's up? |
| KATHIE | I don't know. He just came in with that. |

Kathie points at the hare.

| TOM | Dog must've killed it. |

He crouches and strokes *Sis* a moment.

Poor Sis. Anyone else would've been ever so proud of you.   40

KATHIE	(To *Spider*.) It's alright, love. You don't want to blame yourself, nor Sis. She only did what's natural to a dog. (To *Tom*, whispering.) You best get that thing out of here.
TOM	Wass want me to do with it?
KATHIE	Just get rid of it, bury it, so he can't see it no more.

Tom takes the hare out of the back door.

Let me dry your hair, love.

| SPIDER | Where's big barrit? |
| KATHIE | Dada's going to bury it. |

Spider looks less miserable now that the hare is out of his sight. *Sis* cheers up too and lays her head on his lap.   50

| SPIDER | Sis killed big barrit, Mum. |
| KATHIE | I know. 'Twasn't your fault, 'twasn't her fault. Next time she goes after one, you blow your whistle and she'll come back. Go on, love, you go and get some dry clothes on before tea. |

Spider and Sis go upstairs. Tom comes in with red hands, peering round to check Spider isn't there.

Did you bury it?

TOM	Some of it … the rest is in the larder.
KATHIE	What if he asks what it is when he's eating it?

60

TOM	He never does.
KATHIE	But suppose he does?
TOM	Tell him it's chicken.

Kathie is suddenly desolate.

KATHIE	What's to become of him when we're gone? How will he ever manage on his own?
TOM	Come on, love, we're not that old!

Tom hugs her.

STORYTELLER	Next morning Spider had a nasty cough and a temperature and the doctor was called.

70

The Doctor arrives and spends some time listening to Spider's chest.

DOCTOR	I don't think you've got a lot to worry about. It's just a chill.
TOM	He's never been ill in his life before.
KATHIE	Bit short of breath sometimes, but never what you'd call ill.

They go out and talk on the doorstep.

DOCTOR	You've obviously taken very good care of him. I'd best be off. A few more calls to make. *(Pause.)* Tom, what is your secret with those cabbages?

80

KATHIE	I won't stay for cabbage talk. Goodbye, Doctor.
DOCTOR	Goodbye, Mrs Sparrow.

She goes inside.

TOM   'Tisn't cabbages you want to talk about, is it?

DOCTOR   No, Tom. *(Pause.)* I think it best you should know, your boy
            has a slight heart problem. I didn't want to worry your wife
            with it, but he has what we call a heart murmur.

TOM   Dear God …

DOCTOR   It may be nothing to worry about. If he should show any
            symptoms of trouble with the old ticker in future, we can   90
            have a much more thorough look at him. I shouldn't worry
            your wife about it. Cheerio, Tom … *(Pause.)* Tom?

TOM   Yes. Cheerio.

            Tom *goes indoors.*

KATHIE   What was he on about?

TOM   Oh, just chatting.

STORYTELLER Only Tom knew and only Tom worried. But as harvest time
            came and Spider seemed his usual self once more, some
            days Tom didn't even think about what the doctor had said.

SPIDER   Sis! Come!   100

14 ❖ *Fox and Hounds*

***Percy**, **Billy**, **Ephraim**, **Spider** and **Sis** gather in the stable for the morning* 1
orders.

PERCY   Thistle cutting today, up round Magg's Corner.

                   ***Billy** and **Ephraim** groan and wearily make their way off.*

                   Spider? Come here a minute … you can have the day off
                   today. It's a nice day, and you've worked well this last week,
                   so have a little holiday.

SPIDER   Holiday! Ta, Percy! Sis!

                   ***Spider** sets off as **Mrs Yorke** comes in, dressed for a hunt.*

MRS YORKE   I thought he was happy before he got his dog. He's even   10
                   happier now.

PERCY   Good idea of yours, ma'am.

MRS YORKE   Why, thank you! I do have them occasionally. Percy, I'm
                   having a day's hunting from Bishopstrow. We shan't be
                   coming over this way but I've told Tom to move his sheep
                   nearer home. Better safe than sorry. Who knows which way
                   the fox will take us.

PERCY   Have a good day, ma'am.

MRS YORKE   I shall, I shall.

                   ***Spider** appears, walking joyfully as ever over the Wiltshire   20
                   Downs.*

STORYTELLER   Spider's holiday walk had taken him up to the southern
                   boundary of the farm. Never before had he come this far
                   onto the Downs.

STORYTELLER   Spider had Sis well trained now.

                   ***Spider** whistles to **Sis**.*

If they came across a rabbit or a hare in the fields, Spider could soon bring her to heel.

She comes to his feet.

SPIDER   Good Sis!   30

Spider looks in the holes that honeycomb the hillside.

Barrits' houses.

STORYTELLER   There were hundreds of rabbit holes and, amongst them, one much larger hole.

SPIDER   Vox's house.

The sound of a distant pack of hounds. **Sis** *sniffs the air.*

Dogs …

STORYTELLER   Then he saw a fox coming over the ridge towards him.

*A **fox** appears. The noise of the hounds gets closer.*

SPIDER   Home, Sis. Home!   40

Sis runs off home like a shot.

STORYTELLER   And now the hounds came over the ridge …

SPIDER   Run vox! Run vox! Run!

*The **fox** drags itself past **Spider**, struggling to make the last few yards to its den. **Spider** runs the other way, towards the dogs, holding up his hands.*

Bad dogs! Bad dogs! Bad dogs!

The hounds sweep over him …

*A couple of miles away, **Kathie** comes out into the cottage garden with a basket of washing and finds **Sis**.*   50

KATHIE   Sis? Where's Spider? (*Calling.*) Spider! (*To Sis again.*) Is something wrong? Is he hurt? Tom! Tom!

TOM   What?

KATHIE	Sis came home without Spider. Have you seen him?
TOM	No. Percy said he'd given him the day off. He'll have gone for a walk, I dessay.
KATHIE	But why would he send Sis home ...? Tom, I'm worried. Spider! Spider!
TOM	Don't worry, I'll find him.

*Suddenly **Mrs Yorke** appears on horseback with **Spider** riding behind her, clinging to her waist, whooping with excitement.*   60

KATHIE	Spider!
SPIDER	Spider ride horse, Mum!
KATHIE	Where've you been?
SPIDER	Spider saw vox!
MRS YORKE	Mrs Sparrow, your son ... Lord knows how, he found himself between a fox and the hounds. They were on the verge of killing it. But when we got to him, he was sitting up and the only danger he was in was of being licked to death!
SPIDER	Bad dogs. Mustn't hurt vox. 70
MRS YORKE	If it had been any other boy, I dread to think what might've happened.
TOM	Well, he's not like any other boy, ma'am, thank God.

15 ❖ FIVE O'CLOCK

***Tom**, **Kathie** and **Spider** sit happily side by side on a bench in their garden.*

STORYTELLER	It was 1942. Overseas, battles were fought and men died, but life in the village went on quietly and peacefully as ever.
TOM/KATHIE	*(Finishing singing.)* … happy birthday to you!
STORYTELLER	Spider was sixteen now.

***Kathie** and **Tom** give **Spider** a card and a present.*

KATHIE	Open the card first.
SPIDER	Barrit!
KATHIE	Dada drew it.

***Spider** hugs **Tom**.*

TOM	Now the present.

***Spider** unwraps it.*

SPIDER	Watch! New watch! Ta!
TOM	It's better than the last one.
KATHIE	So you mind how you go with it this time.
SPIDER	Yes, Mama. Spider walk with watch.
KATHIE	Wait! You can wear it round your wrist now like a grown-up, see? *(She fastens the watch round his wrist.)* Now, not too far. You be back in good time for tea, mind.

SPIDER	What time, Dada?
TOM	Well, I got a sick ewe up in the yard as I want to take a look at later. You be there at five o'clock and we'll walk home together.

Tom points at the watchface and counts round the numbers.

One, two, three, four, five. All right?

SPIDER   Sis, come.

Spider goes off with Sis. Tom and Kathie watch him, smiling.

KATHIE   Right. I got washing to do.   30

TOM   What's for tea?

KATHIE   Sausages. Don't be late.

TOM   For sausages? Never.

STORYTELLER   A Sunday it was, and the sun shone warmly from an almost cloudless blue sky, and Spider went to his favourite place ...

Spider comes over the downland with Sis and sits close by the foxhole.

SPIDER   (To Sis.) Go Spider's house. Go on. Spider's house. Spider come soon.

Sis goes. Spider waits. The fox emerges from the den. Then,   40
tentatively at first, two cubs emerge and begin to play. After a little while they dart into the hole again. Spider backs away and stands, speaking softly.

SPIDER   Bye vox.

He goes. The fox goes.

STORYTELLER   Five o'clock came. And went.

Tom washes his hands in a bucket at the sheep pens. He looks at his watch and grins, shaking his head. Then he looks up and listens. Very faintly can be heard the sound of a dog howling.

TOM   Sis?   50

He sets off.

STORYTELLER	The greenness of the spinney was stippled with black, for in every ash tree there sat crows and rooks and jackdaws, still and silent.

Tom arrives at *Spider*'s house, panting hard.

TOM	Spider!

*The birds fly up all at once. **Sis** comes to **Tom** from **Spider**'s house then runs back there and crouches, whining. **Tom** opens the shelter. **Spider** sits inside on the wooden crate, eyes closed as if asleep. Very gently **Tom** takes his hand and finds that it is*   **60** *cold. He listens to his heart but there is no beating. He takes the boy's hand to his face and presses it against his cheek, then takes **Spider** in his arms and holds him tight.*

STORYTELLER	A westerly breeze …
STORYTELLER	… comes over the shoulder of the downs.
STORYTELLER	It ruffles Spider's hair softly against his father's face …
STORYTELLER	… and lifts the crows up high, wheeling over the corn.
STORYTELLER	Down in the valley, the breeze stirs Kathie's washing on the line …
STORYTELLER	… and carries the smell of sausages for tea out over the **70** fields.
STORYTELLER	It blows on and on, tirelessly over the land …
STORYTELLER	… on and away eastwards. On and away.

*One by one, the **Storytellers** walk back over the hill into the wind and the setting sun.*

THE END

ACTIVITIES

THINGS TO TALK ABOUT

1 What expectations does the title *The Crowstarver* seem to set up? If someone you had never met was referred to as a 'crowstarver', what sort of person would you imagine them to be? Does Spider fit in with these expectations? Or is there more to him as a person than someone who would 'have frightened Miss Muffet to death'?

2 It becomes clear early on in the play that Spider isn't like most other boys. Talk about the following:

- What makes Spider an individual?
- What things is he good at doing?
- What do other people do to help Spider live an enjoyable and useful life?
- What does he find difficult?
- What causes him to become unhappy?

3 *The Crowstarver* is set in Wiltshire, a county in the south-west of England, in the 1930s and early 1940s. You may never have been to Wiltshire but take a moment by yourself and, by drawing on things you have seen or read, conjure up a mental picture of the English countryside. Think about any television programmes or films that you have seen that were set in the early part of the last century. How did people dress? What transport did they use? What sorts of job might they have done on the farms?

- In pairs, sit ear to ear but facing away from each other so that you can hear but not see your partner. Imagine your mind is like a film camera that can give a wide angle view or focus in on details. Take it in turns to describe the sort of rural landscape that you think Spider would have lived in.

- Now, focus in on particular parts of the big picture. What sorts of things do you see people doing in the landscape? What do they look like? What are they doing?

- Join up with two other pairs. Look at the way that the Storytellers introduce Scene 1. As a group, devise a sequence in which the Storytellers help the audience see the landscape of *The Crowstarver* in their own minds.

4 The play of *The Crowstarver* is adapted from a novel by Dick King-Smith. Usually, novels are written in the past tense (as if the events took place some time ago) with the author writing as if he or she saw and heard everything that happened. (This is called writing in the third person.)

- Read this extract from the novel:

  > That night she woke some time in the small hours to hear an owl hooting. Beside her, Tom snored softly. The owl, she could hear, was on his usual perch, in the old Bramley apple tree at the bottom of the garden. She waited, half asleep again, for the bird to hoot once more, but when he did, it sounded much closer. It sounded in fact as though it came from the room next door. Spider's room.

- Now reread Scene 3 from where Kathie puts Spider to bed to where she gets him out of his cot (page 7). Talk about how this scene is different from the third-person, past-tense style of the novel.

- Work in pairs. One of you should start telling a simple story in the third person and past tense. For example:

  > One morning a girl called Katie got out of bed. She yawned. She stretched. And she wondered what to have for breakfast.

  Your partner will now 'translate' that into the language of a play. So, it didn't happen to someone else, some time ago (third person, past tense) but it is happening to me, now (first person, present tense). For example:

  > Oh my goodness! Morning already! *(Yawns and stretches.)* Hmmm, what shall I have for breakfast?

  Keep the story going by having one person add just a couple of sentences at a time, and the other acting them out and speaking aloud to describe what they are doing.

5 Another way the play of *The Crowstarver* differs from the original novel is that it *conflates* time. This means that quite large chunks of the novel, in which the author describes things in detail, are squeezed into a short scene. There's no need for a lot of verbal description because the audience can see and hear what's happening.

- Reread the whole of Scene 3 (pages 6–9). Talk about what the audience learns in this one scene about the different characters.

- What challenges does a scene like this present in terms of staging it?

6 Kathie is worried that Spider won't be able to manage the job of scaring the crows because he wouldn't want to frighten the birds. How does Tom manage to get Spider to do the job?

- In pairs, think of a scenario in which a young person has a good reason for not wanting to do something. Examples might be not wanting to walk past a particular house on the way to school because it is supposedly haunted, or not wanting to clean out a pet rabbit's hutch because (a) it stinks, and (b) the rabbit doesn't seem to mind the mess! Write your scenario down on a slip of paper and pass it to another pair of students.

- Read the scenario that is given to you. One of you must become the young person, the other an adult. Improvise the scene in which the adult manages to persuade the young person to just get on with it! The focus here is on use of voice and body language to persuade as well as the words you choose to say.

7 Were you surprised by the way the play ended? How did it leave you feeling? Are the audience given any hints earlier in the play that Spider's life is fragile and his time could stop suddenly?

THINGS TO WRITE ABOUT

8 At the time *The Crowstarver* is set, rural communities tended to be small and close-knit. Most farmworkers lived on or close to a farm in 'tied' cottages owned by the farm owner and successive generations of children followed their parents into farmwork. Playwright Daniel Jamieson writes:

> There was a strong sense of community and people supported each other through adversity, even if some could be small-minded about anything out of the ordinary. In *The Crowstarver*, Dick King-Smith portrays the farm folk with fondness but also candour. The dawning realisation that Kathie and Tom Sparrow's foundling child has learning difficulties is greeted in various ways:
> 'No one said, as they said of their own and each other's children, "He's lovely, ain't he!"
> Everyone thought, some with pity, some without, that it looked as if … Spider was odd." '

- Write a piece of dialogue, of no more than ten lines, between two of the Sparrows' neighbours in which they talk candidly about Spider.

● Now write a ten-line dialogue between one of these neighbours and either Kathie or Tom Sparrow in which they talk about Spider but avoid saying what they really think.

9 Using the playscript as a core source, draw a timeline of Spider's life, noting when significant things happened to him. Now add additional incidents of your own invention that you think would also make interesting scenes in a play about his life.

● Imagine that Kathie and Tom had a photo album that showed important moments in Spider's life. Under each photograph Kathie has written a caption explaining what the snap is showing. Write the captions for six photographs taken at different times in Spider's life.

10 The Storytellers both introduce and close the play of *The Crowstarver*. Some plays, for example *Romeo and Juliet*, begin with a prologue that pretty much tells the audience the story they are about to see acted out. Other plays close with an epilogue that makes a final comment on what the play has shown.

● Working in pairs, write either a prologue or an epilogue for *The Crowstarver* that could be spoken by the Storytellers. One way of doing this would be to use the title of the play as an acrostic, that is, when each letter of the title is used to start each new line. For example:

Tom sits alone in his shepherd's hut.

Hear the lambs crying for their mothers' milk, the

Ewes bleating to calm them.

Can you see through the darkness?

Rolling, empty downland,

Over which stumbles a desolate figure.

What's that she holds so tightly? ...

11 Spider was a special kind of person. Although he was slow at learning many of the things society expects children to learn, he had other talents and a lot of qualities.

A eulogy is a speech or piece of writing that praises someone who has died. Sometimes these are read out at a funeral. Sometimes people prefer to just write something and send it to the relatives of the person who has died.

Imagine you knew Spider. Perhaps you are one of the characters in the play. When you learn that he has died, you feel you need to write something about him to Tom and Kathie.

BRINGING THE PLAY TO LIFE

12 Working in small groups, use the captions you created in Activity 9 to create a sequence of still images that shows Spider's life.

13 It's useful to investigate how characters may be thinking at a particular moment in order to make them seem like real people. Consider, for example, how Spider and Kathie feel about school in Scene 4 (pages 12–14).

- Form two lines facing each other. One line should imagine what Spider is feeling and thinking as his mum takes him to meet Mr Pugh. The other line should imagine what Kathie is thinking and feeling. One person should move slowly down between the two lines. As they pass, each person speaks aloud what is in Kathie's or Spider's mind.

- When this sequence is over, the person should turn around and return down the line. This time everyone says aloud what Kathie and Spider would be thinking and feeling after Mr Pugh has said that Spider isn't suited to school.

14 Nikki Sved, the director of the first production of *The Crowstarver*, notes that the company 'wanted to be as understanding and respectful' as they could be in portraying Spider because 'to get it wrong would be to go against the spirit of the story.' Malcolm Hamilton, who played Spider in Theatre Alibi's second production of the play, said: 'When I was building his character I didn't want his disability to be his defining characteristic. I was more interested in his uniqueness, his affinity with animals, and his particular oddness.'

- Find a space on your own. Look around the space. Imagine that you are seeing it for the very first time. When you feel ready, start to explore the space, holding onto the idea that everything you see and touch is completely new to you (ignore everyone else in the group, just pretend you are entirely alone).

- Develop a way of moving from one part of the room to another. Find a way of feeling, smelling and listening to things that is idiosyncratic (that is, it belongs only to you).

- Create a character of your own like Spider by developing a short sequence which illustrates the particular way the character moves, something the character does with great care, and something in particular the character says. The aim of this exercise is to create a sequence that will make the audience interested in the character without mocking him or her.

15 *The Crowstarver* presents a number of exciting challenges – not least, how to portray the various animals. Here's how Theatre Alibi approached the problem:

> Rather than trying too hard to play all the physical attributes of the animal (crouching, running on all fours etc.), the actors concentrated on the personality of each animal and played them almost like other human characters.
>
> When depicting these animals, the actors found that showing one or two physical attributes suggested their bodily presence better than a complete impersonation. For example, when playing the dogs they would slap their thighs to suggest their tails wagging. The horses tended to stamp impatiently and toss their heads. Noises helped too, of course.

- Working in small groups, choose a domestic or farmyard animal. Imagine the animal as a person and jot down words that would describe its character. A good way of getting started is to think about binary opposites: for example, when you think of the animal do you think big or small, heavy or light, fast or slow, clever or stupid, good or bad?

- Think of as many binary opposites as you can for your chosen animal. The next challenge is to use your selected words to develop physical characteristics. Experiment with facial expressions and ways of moving that fit your words.

- Try now to add an individual personality to your animal by developing a few key gestures. For example, a cat might prowl, moving lightly on its feet and displaying a crafty expression. In terms of personality, it could seem haughty, holding its nose in the air in a moment of stillness as if to look down on all the other animals in the yard. In the original production, the bronco was played as if he were a proud, raging prizefighter who tossed his head as if shaking a long mane of shiny hair from his eyes.

- Give your animal two or three sounds. The cat, for example, might either purr softly or hiss spitefully, the bronco might stamp impatiently or whinny threateningly.

- Having developed your animal with the help of your group, move around the room in character. Take your time with this. How does your animal respond to others? There should be no human talk in this exercise, though the animals should make it very clear how they feel about each other through the way they move, gesture and make sounds.

16 Another way to portray some of the animals would be through the use of puppets. Look at these two pictures from the original production.

Notice how the designer (Trina Bramman) has concentrated on key characteristics of the animals, rather than attempting to make the puppets look completely naturalistic. You will also see how each puppet needs a number of actors to work together to give it movement.

● Work in pairs or threes. You will need several large sheets of newspaper and some sticky tape. Find a way of making a simple animal puppet from the newspaper. It will be fine so long as it has a body, four legs, a head and perhaps ears and a tail, if those are important features of your chosen animal.

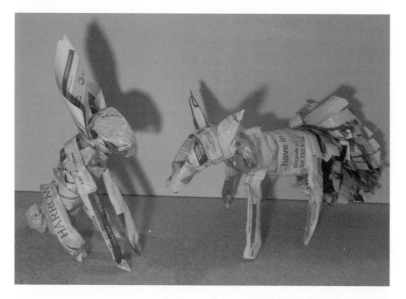

● Now you need to bring your animal to life. Start by imagining that it is sleeping and the only movement it makes is breathing. How does the animal wake up? Let it have a stretch, bring it up onto all four legs, give it a look around to check the environment and then move it forward just a few steps. This will take a fair deal of time and patience but stick with it and you will be amazed at how lifelike your newspaper puppet can become. One thing you must remember is to keep the puppet moving all the time even if the movement is very, very slight.

● Take a look at the video clip of Spider and the fox on Theatre Alibi's website (www.theatrealibi.co.uk).

17 Performing the animals isn't the only challenge *The Crowstarver* presents that could be tackled through a physical theatre approach. Experiment with how you might show:

- Percy giving Spider a ride on his motorbike (page 24)
- the plane dogfight and Spider nearly being hit by the German fighter (pages 29–30)
- the foxhounds sweeping over Spider (page 46)
- Mrs Yorke bringing Spider home on her horse (page 47).

18 In Dick King-Smith's novel *The Crowstarver*, Percy tells Major Yorke about a time when Spider was chased over the fields by a group of boys barking at him like a pack of hounds and pushing his face into a cowpat when they caught him. Playwright Daniel Jamieson thought this was a particularly significant moment and chose to work it into the stage production.

- Read Scene 5 again (pages 15–18).
- Why do you think this is a particularly significant scene? What does it say about the different attitudes people have towards Spider?
- What effect do you think the incident has on Spider? Does it affect what he does after the experience?
- In groups, devise another scene in which the way people treat Spider has an effect on what he does in the future.

STAGING THE PLAY

19 Look back at the cast list on page IX. In the original production of *The Crowstarver* there were just five actors. Rather than seeing this as a disadvantage, Nikki Sved, the director, explains how it added something to the play:

> Theatre Alibi is a company of storytellers. Nobody's in character at the start of the show and you see each actor gradually taking on characters. Women become men, humans become animals, people become other people. When you see an actor taking on a character, you clearly witness an act of empathy. That adds something rich to the equation, watching an attempt to understand someone. I think to see that transition is of worth in itself.

- This is a good artistic reason for only having a few actors. What would be the other advantages for a professional company of having just a small number of actors?

- Look again at page IX, which shows how Theatre Alibi *doubled* the parts (that is, arranged it so that a number of parts could be played by the same actor). Are there any parts that you think it would be a mistake to double? If your group was to perform *The Crowstarver*, how would you double the parts?

20 In the novel *The Crowstarver*, the farm owner is a man, Major Yorke. Theatre Alibi changed the character into Mrs Yorke. Why do you think they did this? Do you think the decision adds new qualities to the drama?

- In pairs, mixed boy and girl if possible, choose one of the following scenes between Mrs Yorke and Percy to work on:
  - Scene 5 (page 15)
  - Scene 6 (pages 19–20)
  - Scene 10 (pages 33–34).

- Think about the status relationship between the two characters. In what ways does Mrs Yorke have more status than Percy? Are there any ways in which Percy has greater status than Mrs Yorke? Are they similar in any ways? Rehearse one of the scenes above and try to make this complex status relationship apparent in the way the characters speak and respond to each other.

21 Some stage directions give very precise instructions to different members of the production team. For example, the playwright might want a particular lighting or sound effect to suggest a certain mood or symbolic meaning. Perhaps the way one character looks at another needs to be specified in order to tell the audience something about their relationship.

- Discuss the importance of these stage directions and try out how they could be achieved:

  A storm lantern sheds a golden glow. (page 1)

  Kathie and **Spider** *walk on their way.* **Mrs Yorke** *watches for a while.* (page 11)

  Tom *realises what he's said, to* **Percy** *of all people.* (page 33)

- Sometimes playwrights are content to leave actors and directors to work out their own way of achieving an effect. A famous example of this is in Peter Shaffer's play *The Royal Hunt of the Sun,* in which one stage direction reads: '*The men climb the Andes. It is a terrible progress; a stumbling, tortuous climb into the clouds, over ledges and giant chasms.*'

  Experiment with ways of bringing the following stage directions to life:

  April 1926. A moonlit night on a windswept hillside. Straggling figures walk over the brow and stop before us, listening to the night sounds. They begin to tell us a story … (page 1)

  Kathie *neatens his hair fondly. A flock of lapwings lifts out of a nearby field with mournful cries.* (page 10)

  He leans out over the parapet to see where it has gone, loses his balance and falls in after it. He goes under for a moment, then bobs to the surface, screaming. (page 32)

22 Choose one or two scenes from the play and consider how music and sound effects could be used to create mood and atmosphere.

- In groups, experiment with ways of using your own voices and bodies to generate sounds effects, for example:

  Suddenly all the pigeons lift off at once. (page 24)

  It starts to rain. (page 25)

  The noise of the hounds gets closer. (page 46)

- For the original production of *The Crowstarver,* Theatre Alibi commissioned Thomas Johnson to compose the music. Here he describes how he started the job:

  > The importance of the landscape is really there in the book and I wanted to put it in the play. So, I was trying to create a very English, pastoral, turn-of-the-century quality, with references to Elgar and Vaughan Williams. The music is very often trying to paint big, broad landscape pictures. A lot of the time I was trying to imagine how it might look as a film, how the dialogue might sound in that context, so the music is often trying to get that wide-angle feel. You've got huge countryside, big hills, big skies, crows in the trees. Also, the book and the play very much feel about the seasons passing, mankind's place inside nature and the cycle of life. Those are the big themes that the music is trying to pursue.

Listen to music such as Vaughan Williams' 'The Lark Ascending' or 'Fantasia on Greensleeves' and Edward Elgar's 'Cello Concerto in E Minor, Opus 85' and you'll get the idea.

23 A number of different locations are mentioned in *The Crowstarver* and the action moves rapidly from one place to another. Building and changing elaborate sets for all of these would be expensive, impractical and slow the production down too much, so you would need to think of other ways of suggesting these locations.

- Draw up a table such as the one below and make notes on how each scene might be simply but effectively suggested.

Scene	Location	Stage furniture / Props / Lighting / Sound
1	Tom's lambing shed	

- Another possible way of suggesting different scenes would be to project captions or pictures of the locations behind the actors. Select a section of the play and construct a PowerPoint sequence that could be used as a backdrop to the action. Discuss the advantages and disadvantages of such a method.

EXPLORING THE ISSUES

24 Spider appears to have some sort of learning disability. What other plays, films, television shows and novels do you know of that feature characters with disabilities? Working in a group, draw up a table like the one below and list them.

Films	TV shows	Plays	Novels

If the only experience you had of people with disabilities and special needs came from these fictional representations, what conclusions would you draw about them? Create a spider diagram to collect your thoughts.

People with disabilities and special needs are ...

Think about people you know who have some sort of physical or learning disability. To what extent do the fictional representations you have noted match your actual personal experience?

25 The 2012 Paralympic Games in London saw over 4,000 disabled athletes from 167 countries competing. In the UK alone, nearly 11 million people watched Professor Stephen Hawking, who has been described as the most famous disabled person in the world, speak at the opening ceremony. The ethos of the Paralympics is to focus on what people can do rather than what they can't do. The London 2012 Games were generally regarded as a tremendous success in helping to develop positive attitudes towards people who are, in one way or another, disabled. Nonetheless, it may be that there is still a good deal of confusion, ignorance and prejudice about disability. There are over 10 million people in the UK who may be considered as disabled. That's almost 20 per cent of the population. The chances are that, if you are not disabled yourself, you will have family members, neighbours or go to school with people who are. Despite this, 40 per cent of people who are not disabled claim that they don't know anyone who is!

- What picture do you see in your mind when you think of a disabled person?
- Can you always see someone's disability?
- Would you say that Spider was a disabled person?

26 According to The Children's Act (1989) a child is disabled if he or she: '... is blind, deaf or dumb or suffers from a mental disorder of any kind or is substantially and permanently handicapped by illness, injury or congenital deformity or such other disability as may be prescribed.'

In schools, it is recognised that many young people have a special educational need. Some of these might be linked to physical disabilities or a mental impairment but they might also come about because of difficulties with thinking and learning things; emotional, behavioural and social difficulties; and difficulties in communicating and interacting with other people.

● What reasons might there be for people to experience these kinds of difficulties?

● What sorts of thing could help people manage or even overcome some of these kinds of difficulties?

● What sort of things would make dealing with them even more difficult?

27 In Scene 4 (page 12) some local boys mock Spider but quickly stop when Kathie sees them. In Scene 5 (pages 16–17) they go to Spider's cottage, presumably with the sole intention of teasing and bullying him.

Research shows that young people with special educational needs or disabilities are significantly more likely to be bullied. In fact, 83 per cent of young people with learning difficulties report that they have experienced bullying in the form of:

– being verbally or physically abused

– being threatened and intimidated

– being excluded from the group

– being manipulated and made to do things they don't want to do

– having their belongings stolen or hidden

– becoming victims of 'false friendship' (that is, when peers act as if they were the person's friend when people are looking but behave spitefully when others, particularly teachers or other figures in authority, are not there to witness their cruelty).

- How would you want an audience to feel about the boys in Scenes 4 and 5? This is called positioning the audience.

- Create a scene of your own that illustrates how someone might be bullied. Before you start to devise the scene, decide what you want the audience to think and feel about the bullies and the bullied. Keep this aim in mind throughout both the devising process and the performance.

- Share your scenes and discuss how effective they were in terms of:

  a illustrating different kinds of bullying

  b positioning the audience towards the bullies and the bullied

  c changing attitudes.